Other cartoon giftbooks in this series:

The Fanatic's Guide to Cats
The Fanatic's Guide to Computers
The Fanatic's Guide to Dads
The Fanatic's Guide to Golf
The Mobile Phone Cartoon Book

The Fanatic's Guide to Husbands
The Fanatic's Guide to Love
The Fanatic's Guide to D.I.Y.
The Fanatic's Guide to Sex

This hardback edition published simultaneously in 1998 by
Exley Publications Ltd. in Great Britain, and
Exley Publications LLC in the USA.

12   11   10   9   8   7   6   5   4

Printed in China.

Exley Publications Ltd, 16 Chalk Hill, Watford, Herts, WD19 4BG, United Kingdom.
Exley Publications LLC, 185 Main Street, Spencer, MA 01562, USA.
www.helenexleygiftbooks.com

Young
at
heart

CARTOONS BY
ROLAND FIDDY

 **EXLEY**

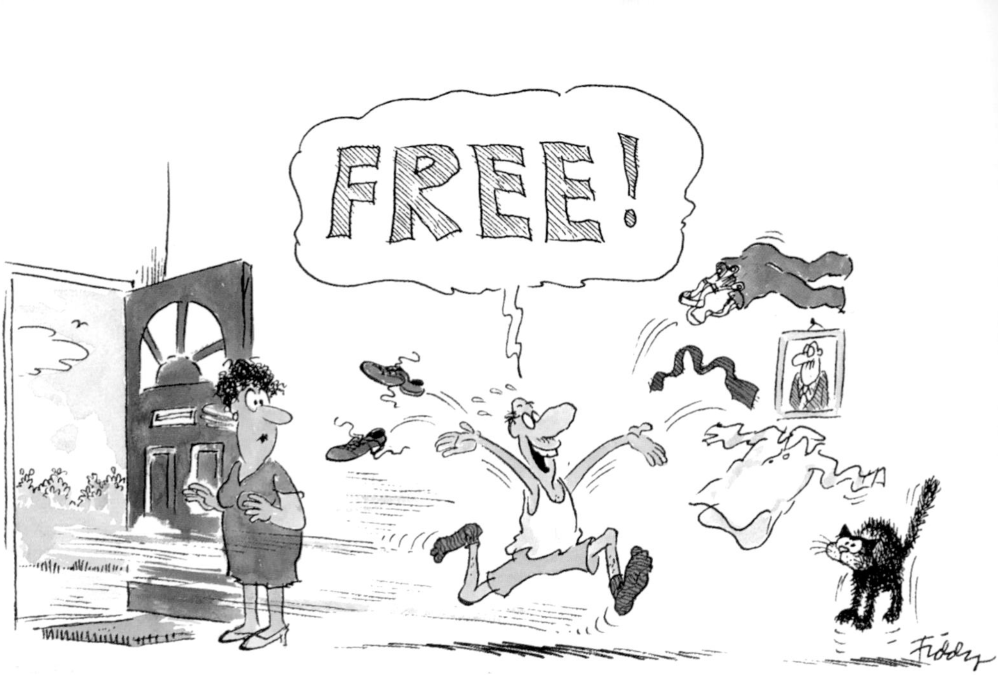
FREE!
Fiddy

THIS IS JUST THE BEGINNING!

THERE IS NO LONGER ANY NEED TO BE A CONFORMIST.
YOU ARE FREE TO EXPERIMENT! . . . . .

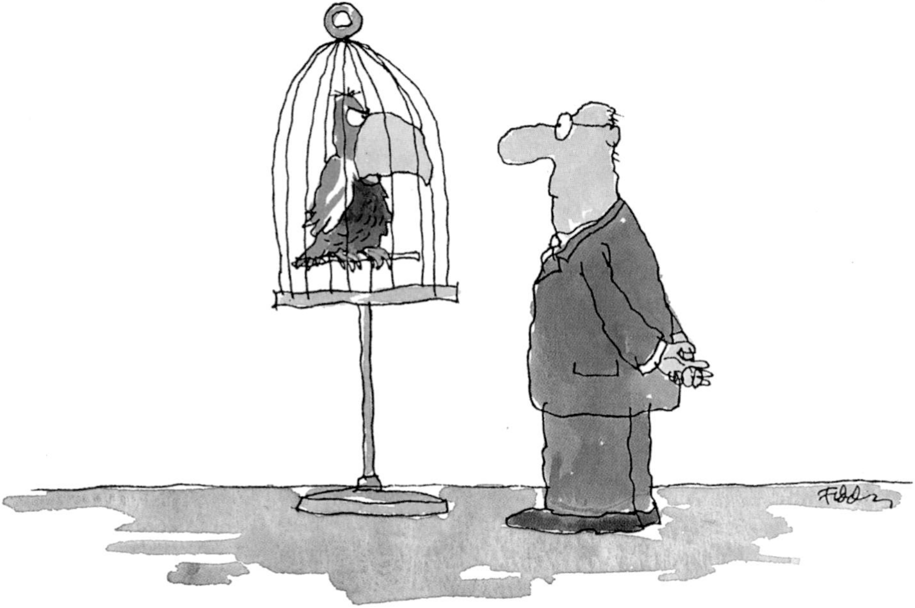

YOU COULD BECOME A BIRDWATCHER...

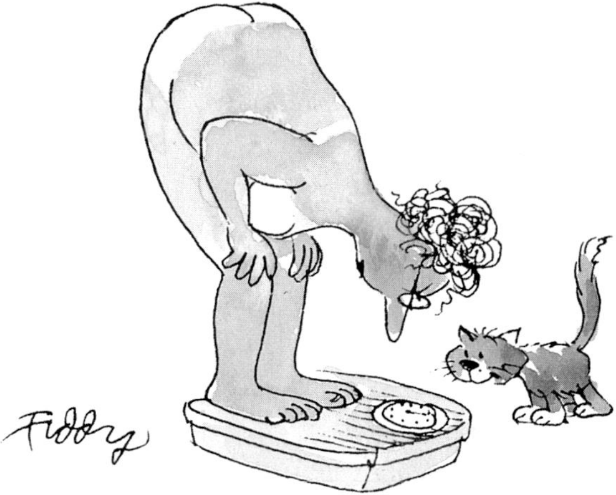
Fiddy

. . . A WEIGHT WATCHER

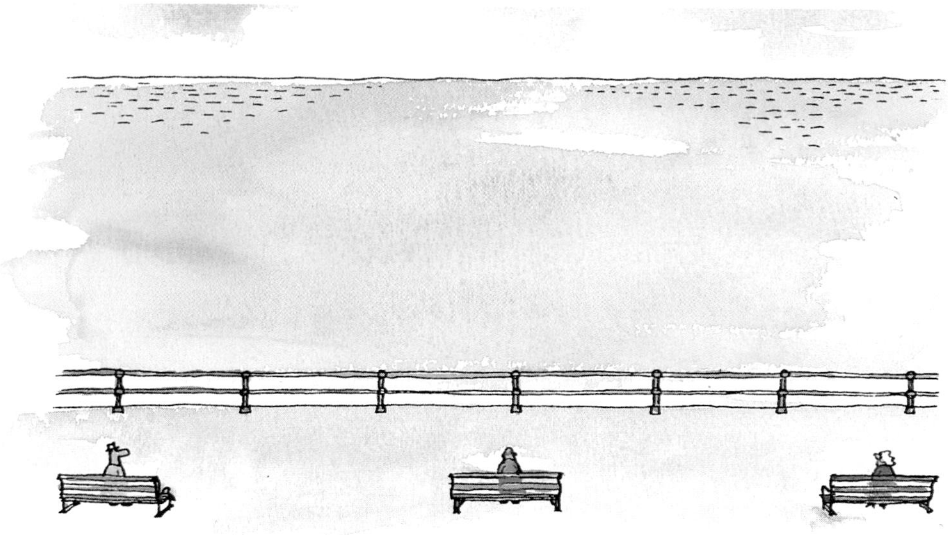

...A SEA WATCHER,...

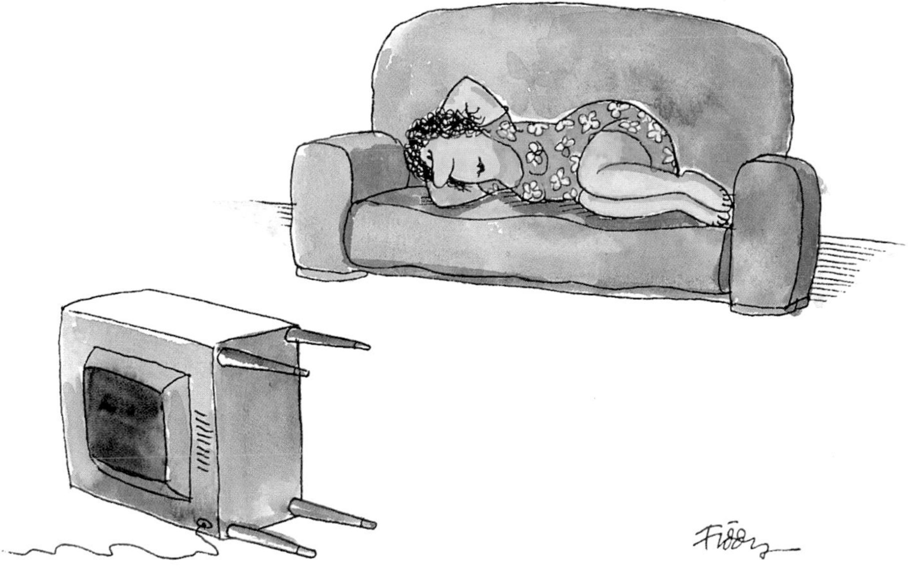

. . . OR A TELEVISION WATCHER,

.... A MARATHON WALKER ...

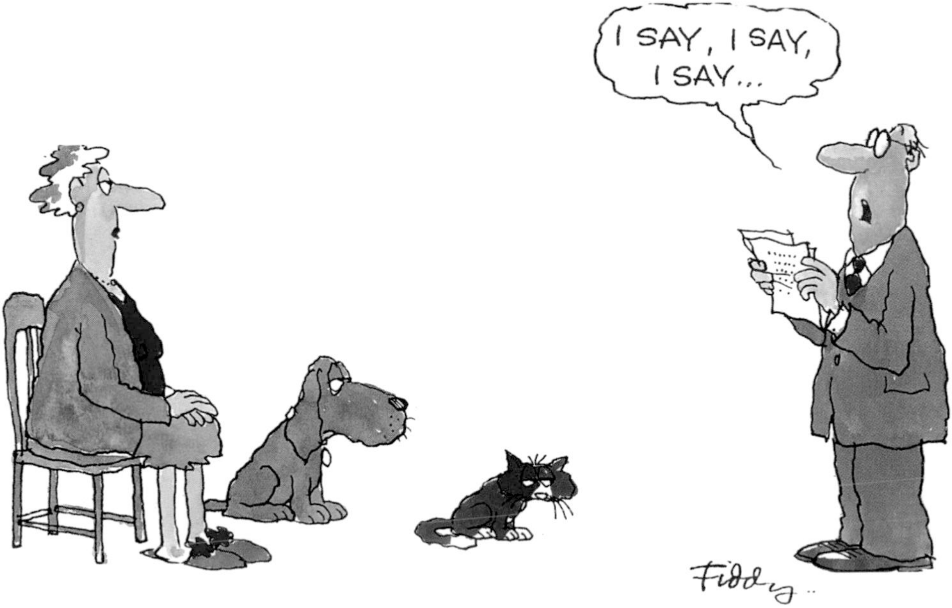
I SAY, I SAY,
I SAY...
Fiddy

A COMEDIAN.

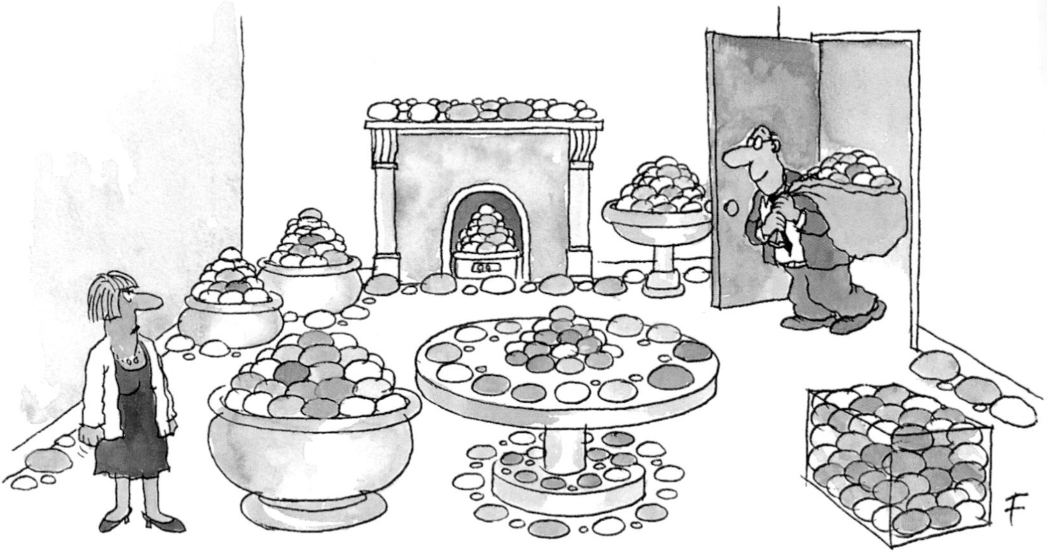

COLLECT PEBBLES

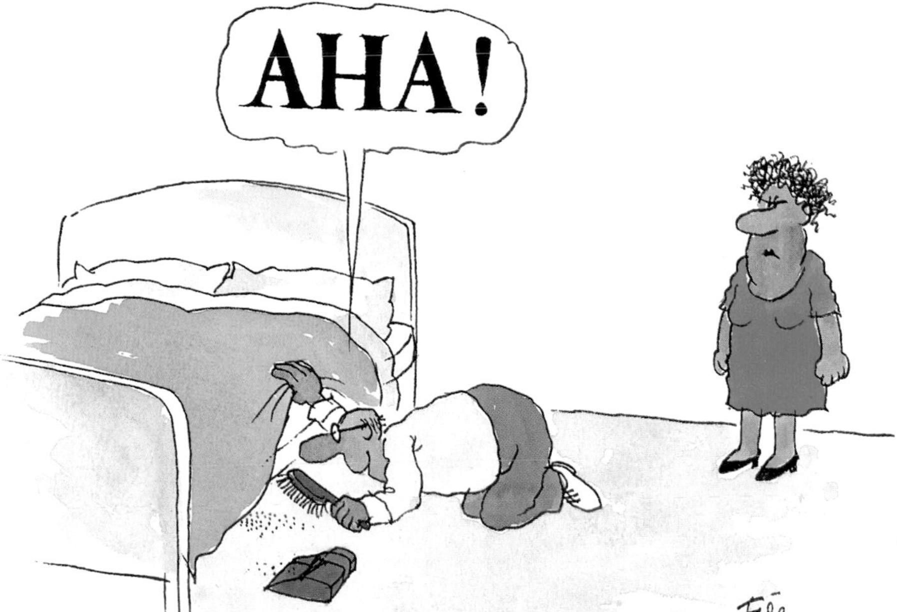
AHA!

SEARCH FOR DUST

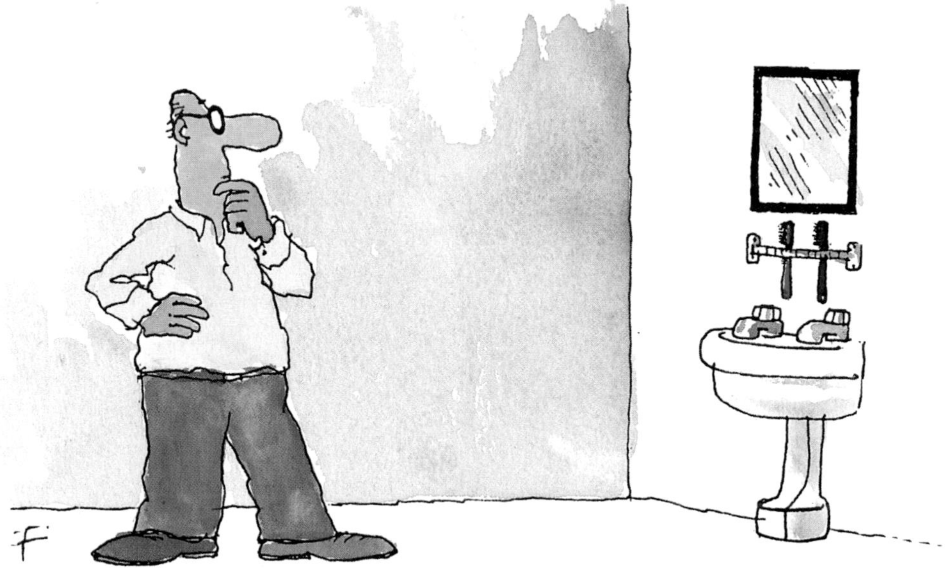

REARRANGE THE TOOTHBRUSHES

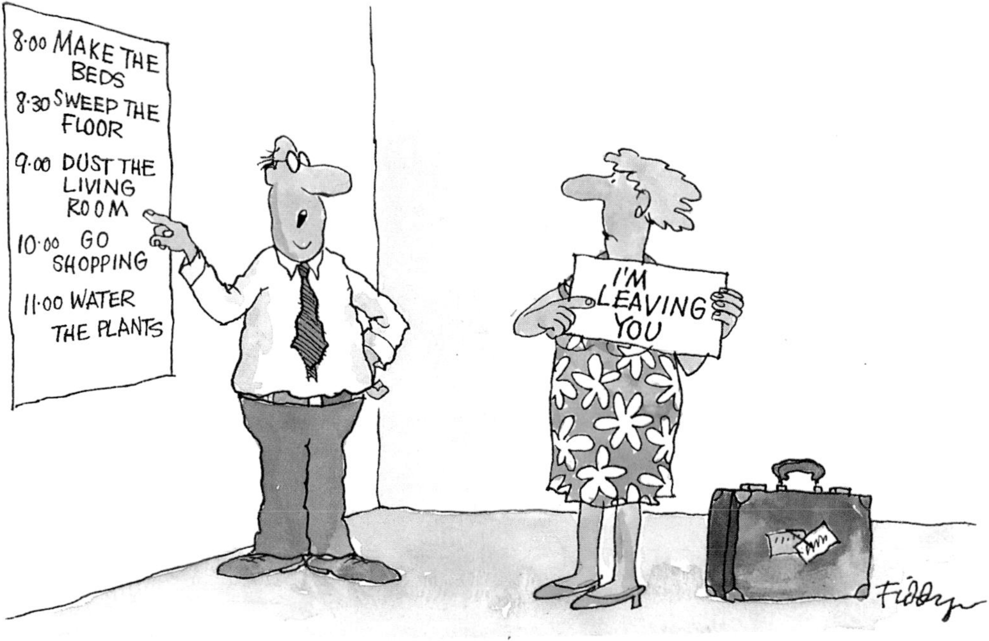
8·00 MAKE THE BEDS
8·30 SWEEP THE FLOOR
9·00 DUST THE LIVING ROOM
10·00 GO SHOPPING
11·00 WATER THE PLANTS
I'M LEAVING YOU

REORGANISE THE DOMESTIC CHORES

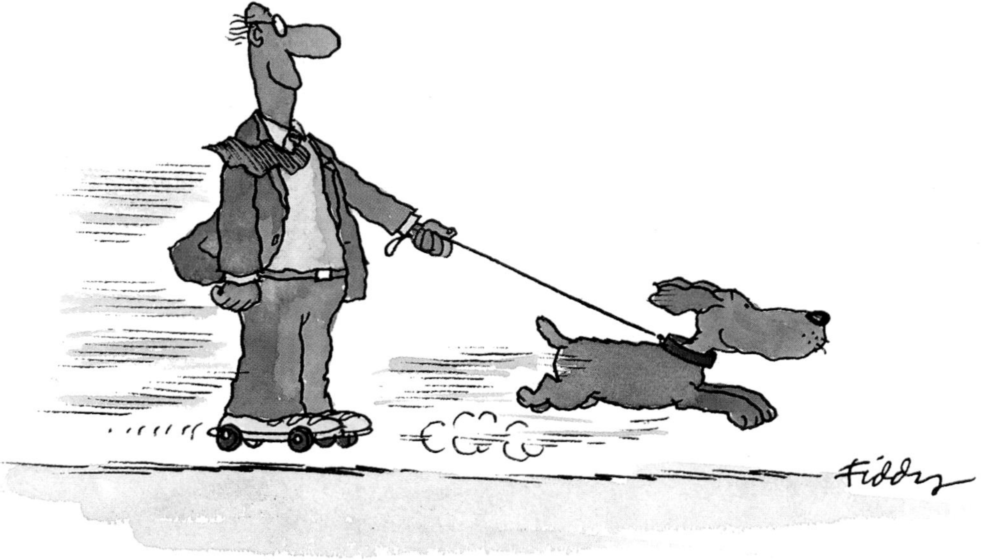
Fiddy

KEEP FIT!

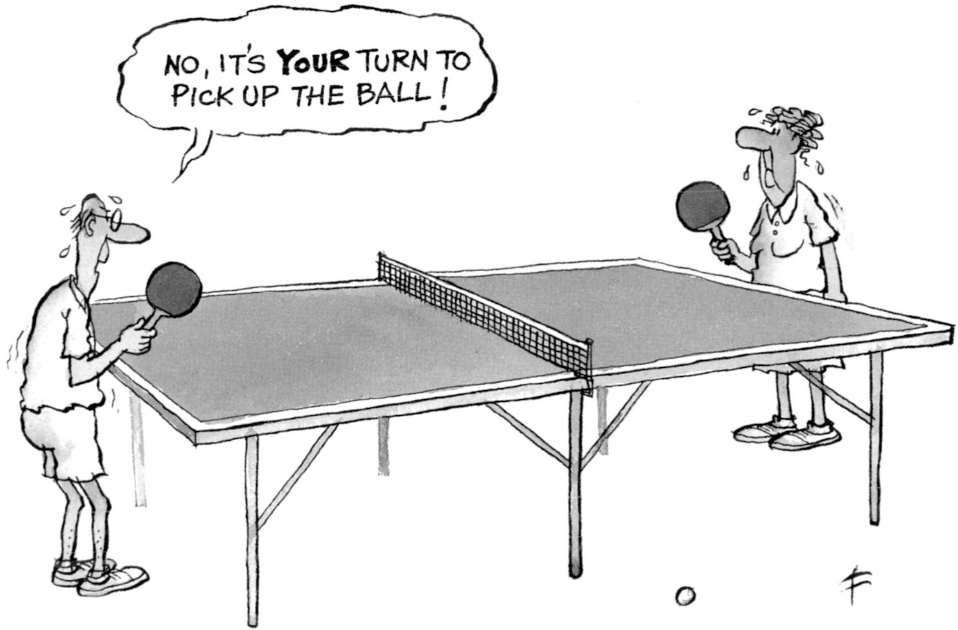
NO, IT'S YOUR TURN TO PICK UP THE BALL!

... TAKE UP PING-PONG

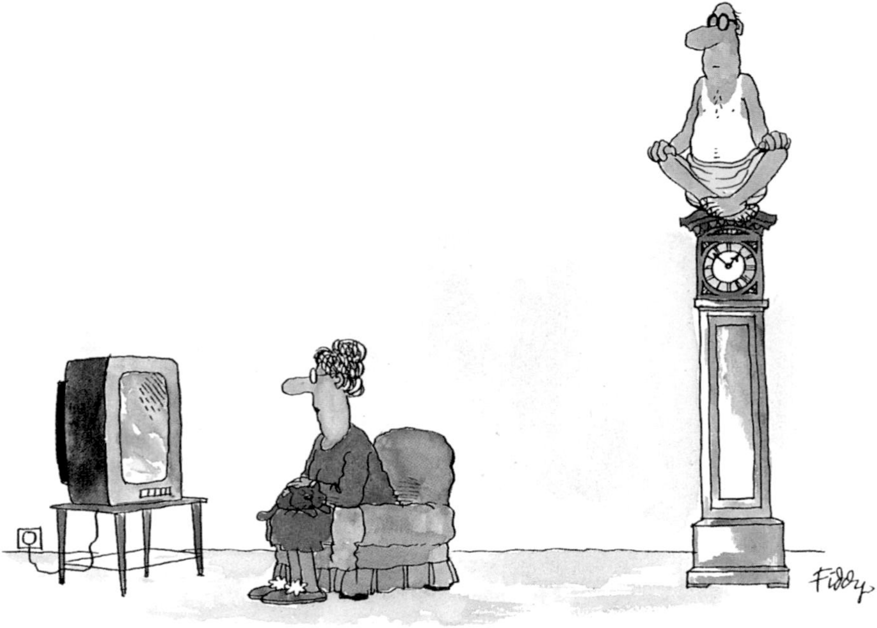
Fiddy

TAKE UP MYSTICISM.

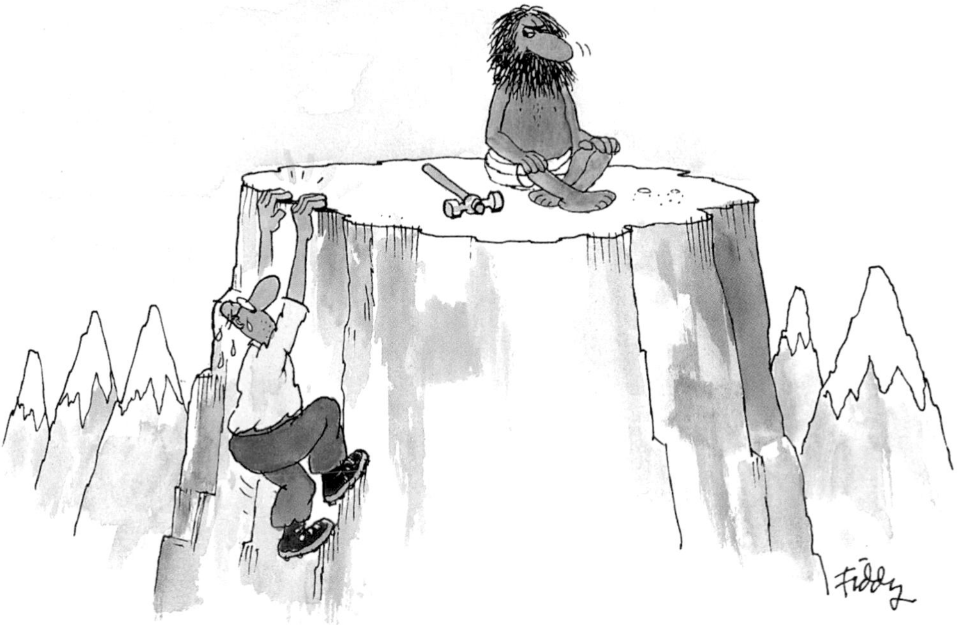
Fiddy

GO AND SEARCH FOR THE MEANING OF LIFE.

YOU'RE FREE TO CHANGE

YOUR LIFESTYLE...

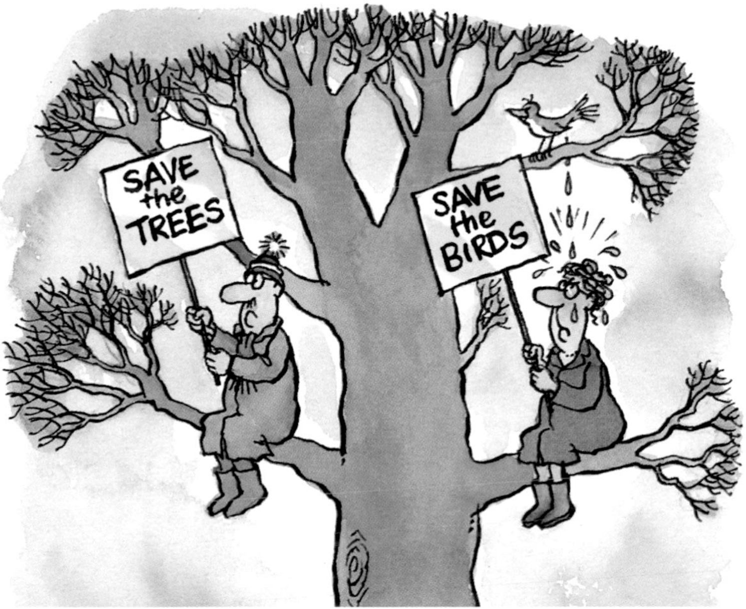
SAVE the TREES
SAVE the BIRDS

DEMONSTRATE FOR THE PROTECTION OF THE ENVIRONMENT...

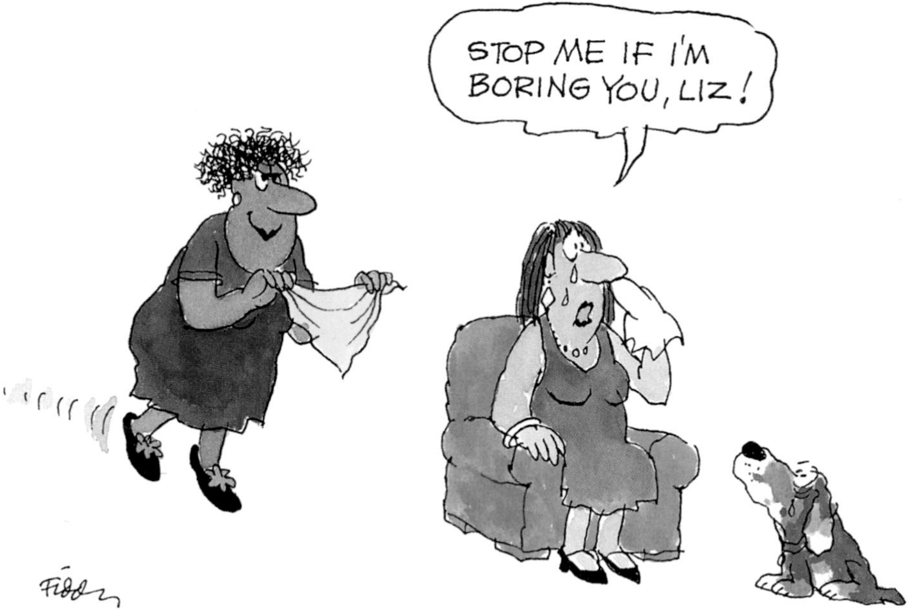
STOP ME IF I'M BORING YOU, LIZ!

BE A GOOD LISTENER...

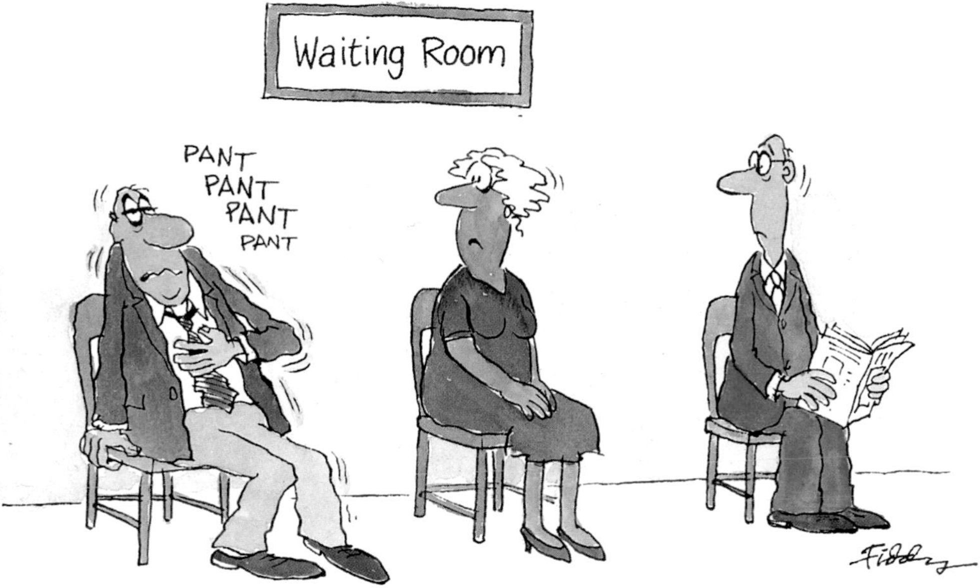
Waiting Room
PANT
PANT
PANT
PANT

SIT IN THE DOCTOR'S WAITING ROOM
AND MAKE EVERYBODY UNEASY.

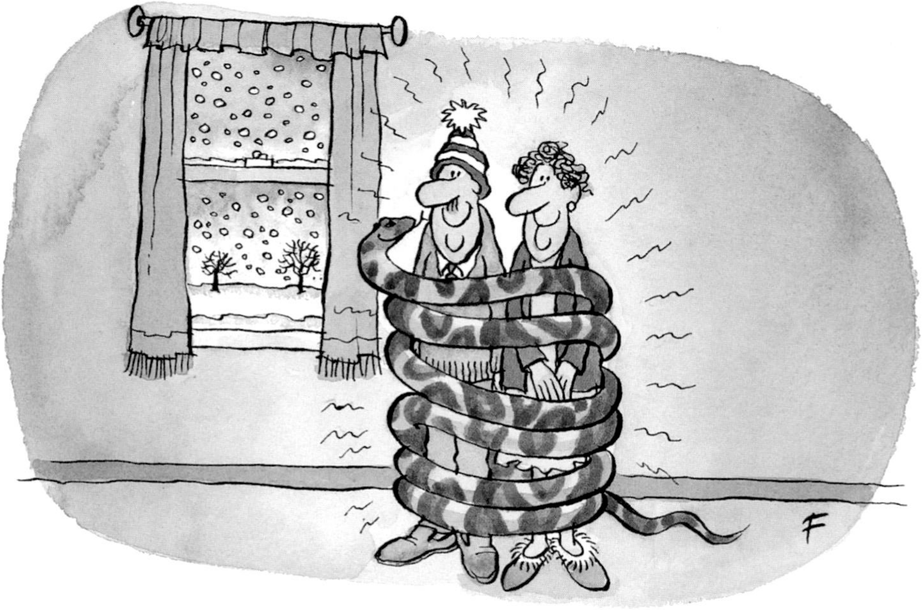
F

KEEP WARM DURING THE WINTER MONTHS.

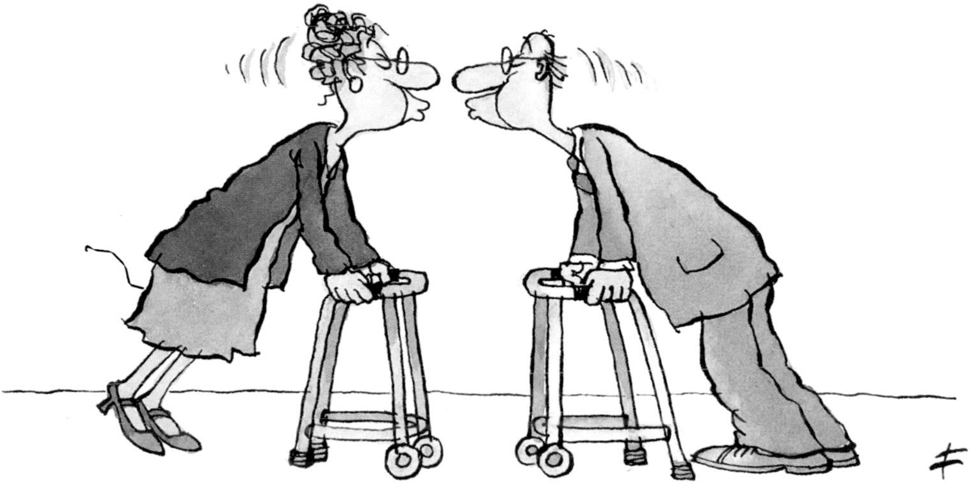

FALL IN LOVE AGAIN...

YOU CAN ADOPT A WEE PET...

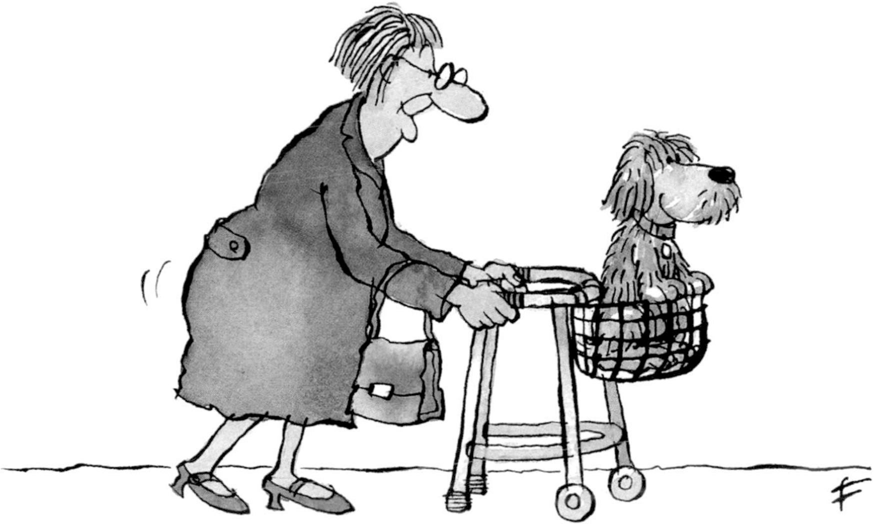

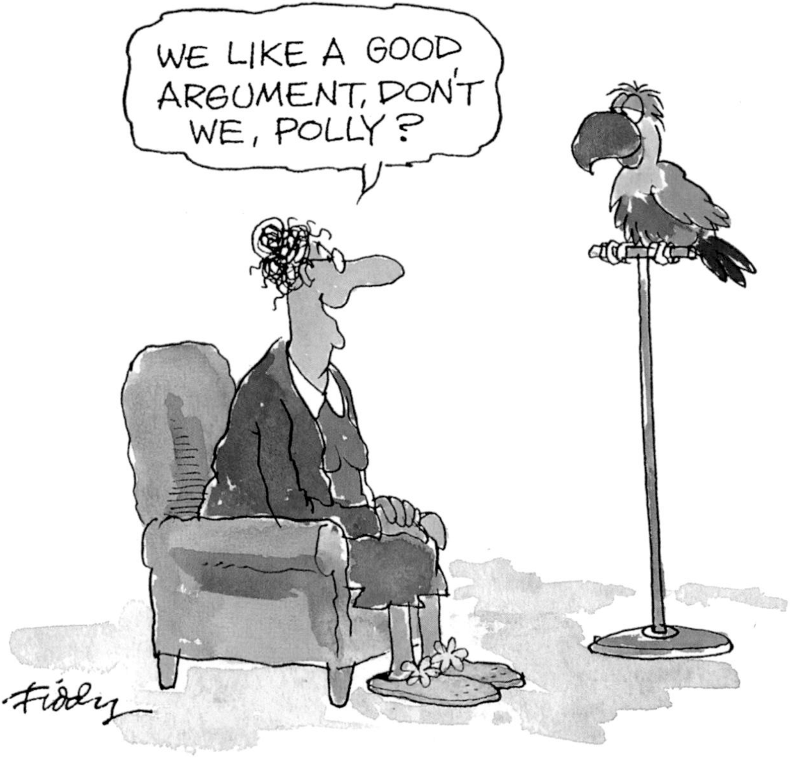
WE LIKE A GOOD ARGUMENT, DON'T WE, POLLY?
Fiddy

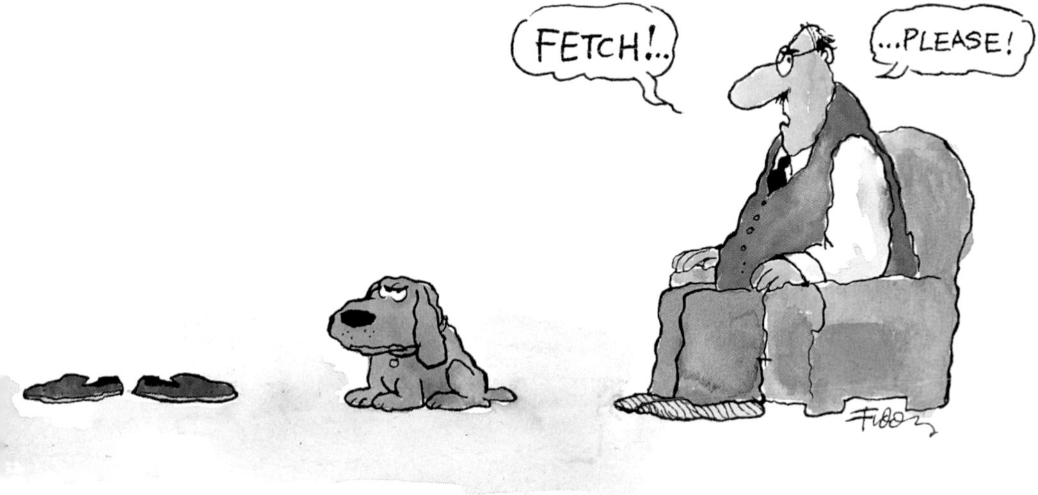
FETCH!..
...PLEASE!

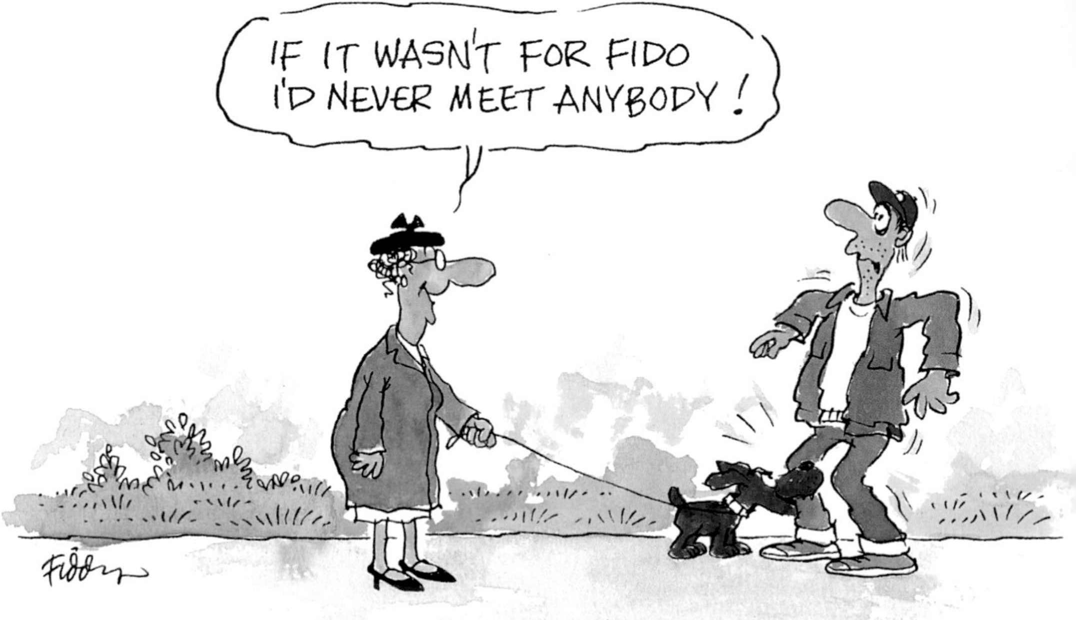
IF IT WASN'T FOR FIDO I'D NEVER MEET ANYBODY!

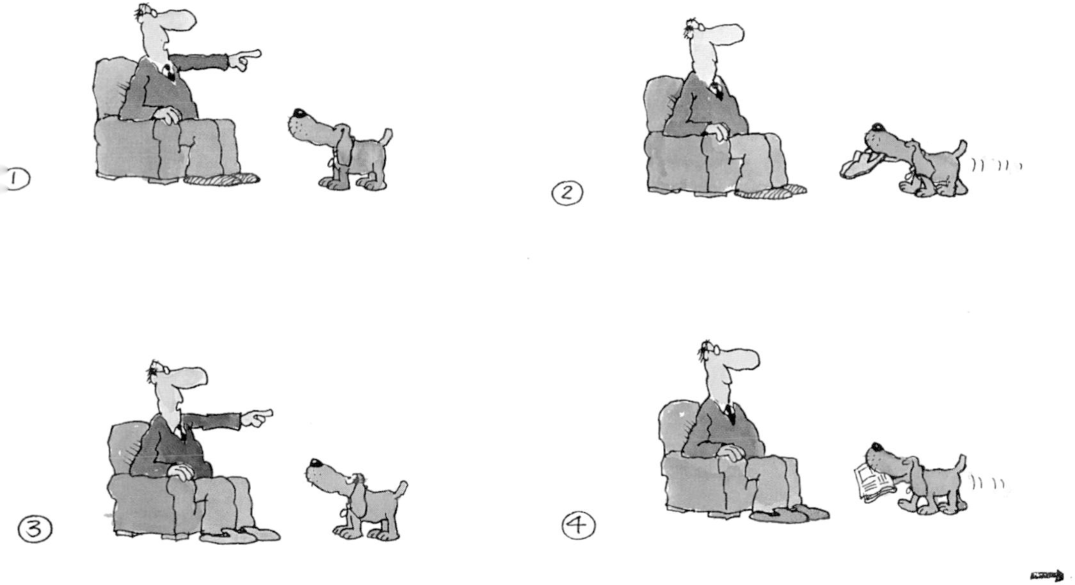

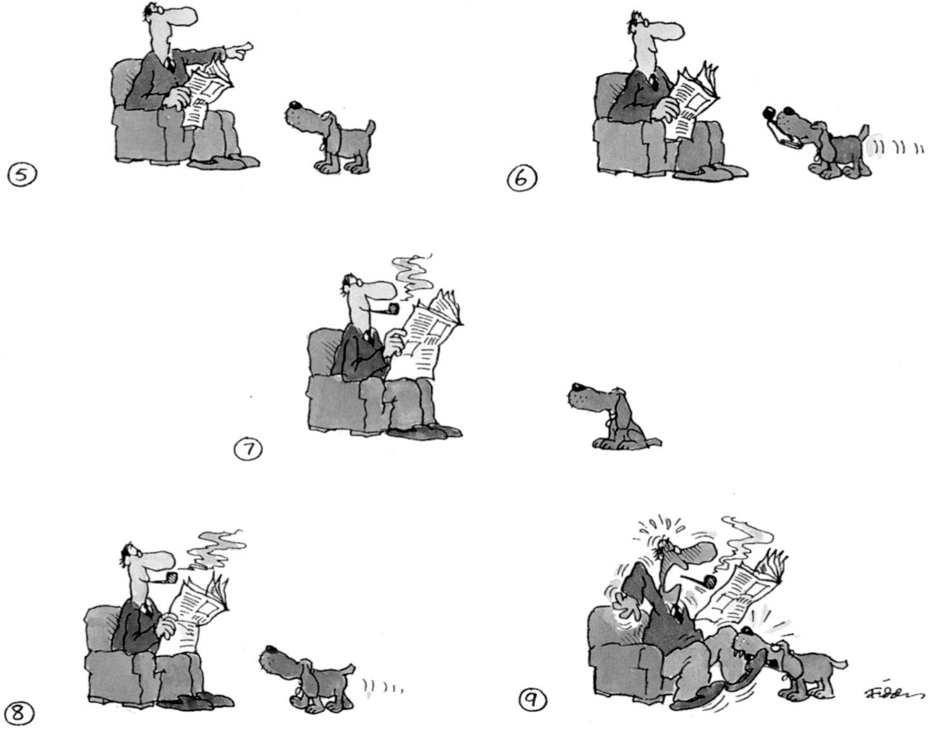
5
6
7
8
9

IT IS IMPORTANT

TO KEEP YOURSELF IN SHAPE...

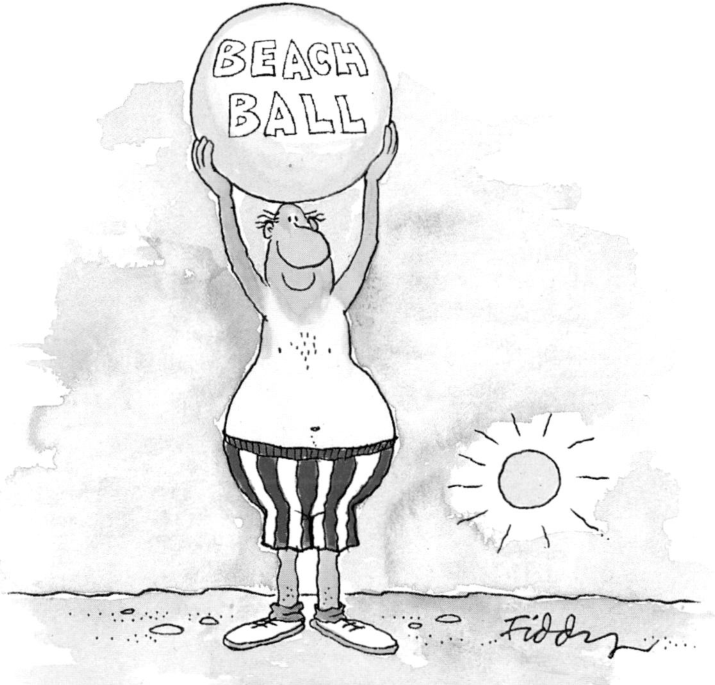
BEACH
BALL

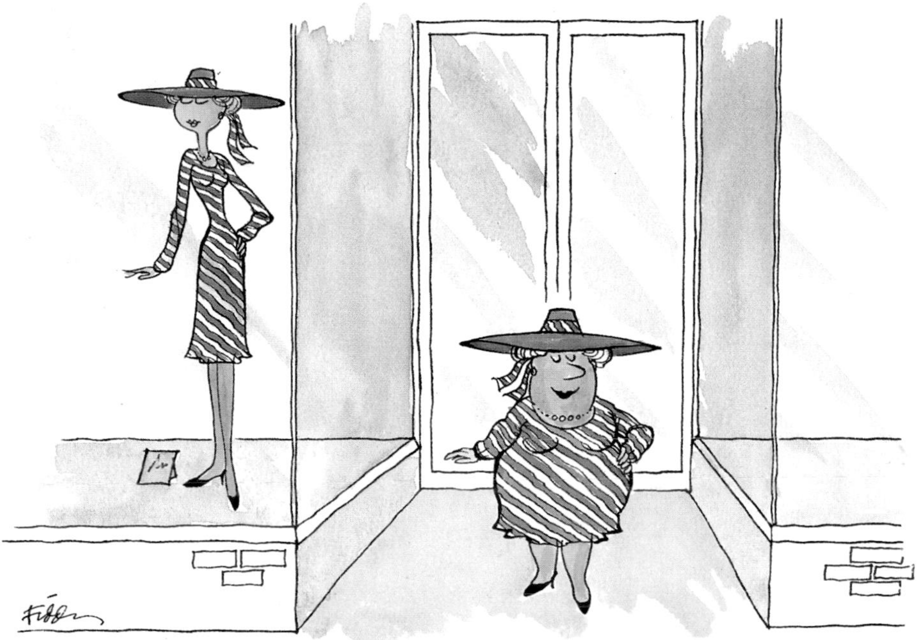

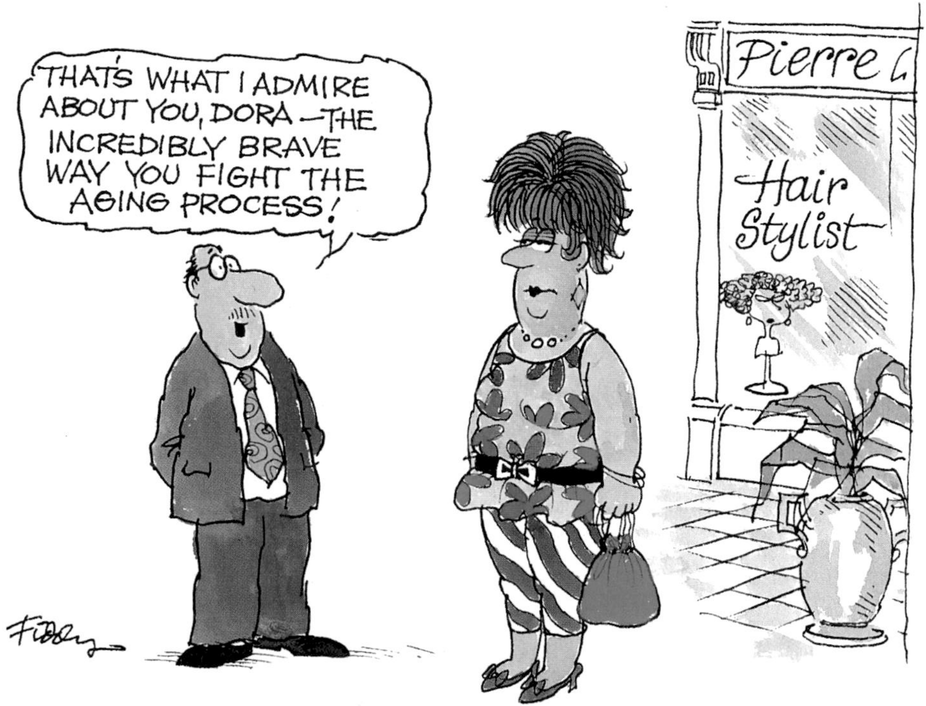
THAT'S WHAT I ADMIRE ABOUT YOU, DORA — THE INCREDIBLY BRAVE WAY YOU FIGHT THE AGING PROCESS!
Pierre
Hair Stylist

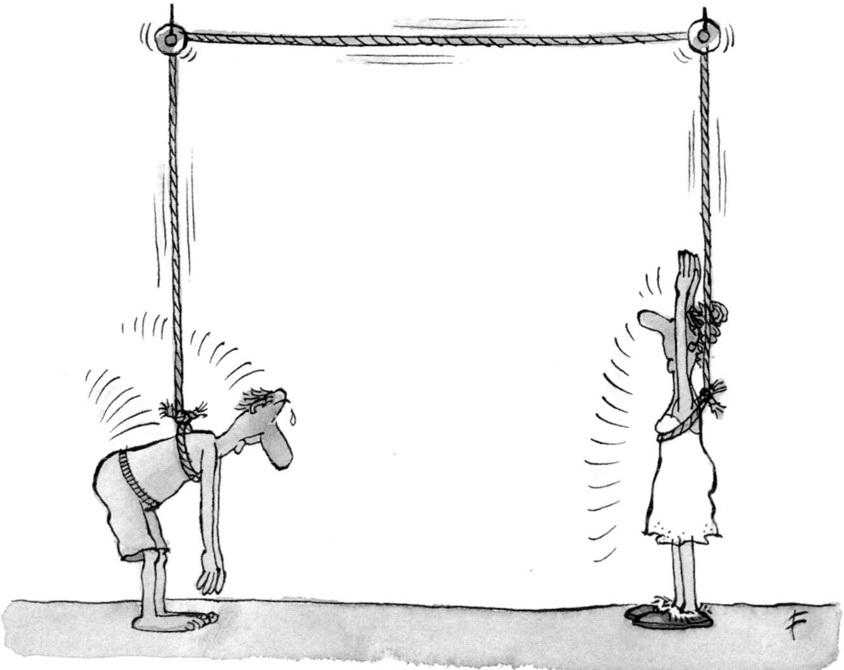

YOU COULD BECOME A FITNESS FIEND...

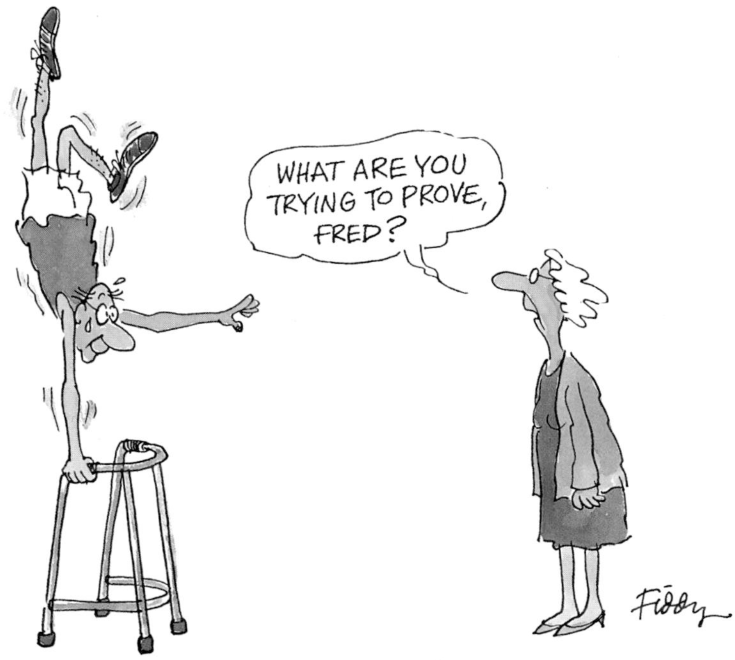
WHAT ARE YOU TRYING TO PROVE, FRED?
Fiddy

OFFER TO TAKE CARE

OF THE KIDS...

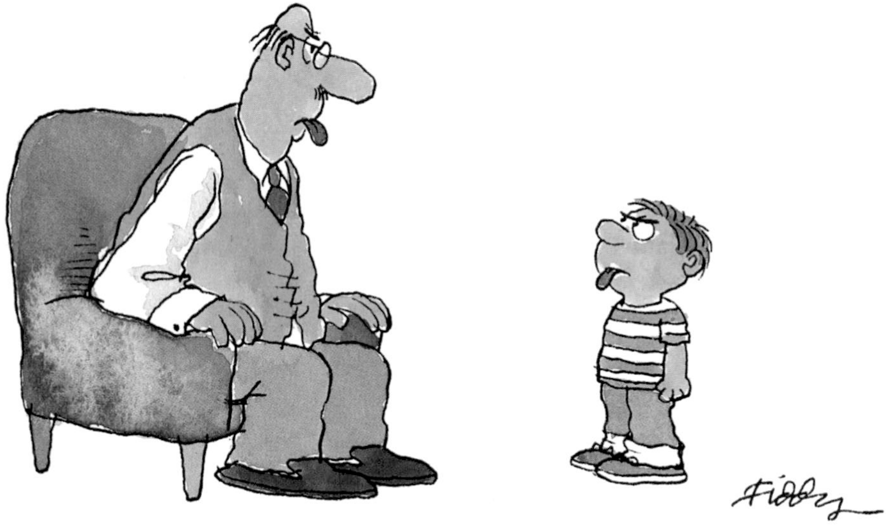

TEACH YOURSELF TO COMMUNICATE WITH THE YOUNGER GENERATION AT THEIR OWN LEVEL.

KEEP UP WITH THE GRANDKIDS

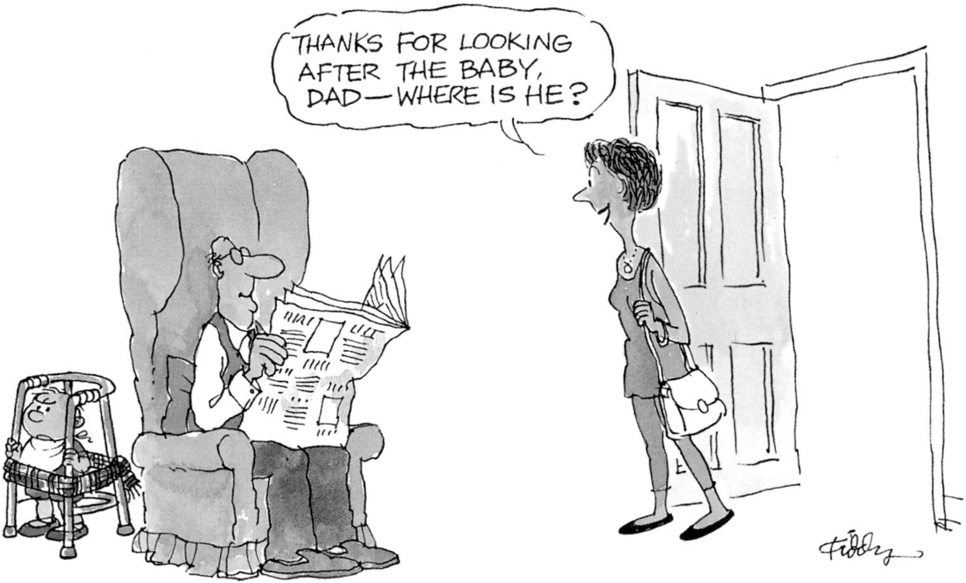
THANKS FOR LOOKING AFTER THE BABY, DAD—WHERE IS HE?

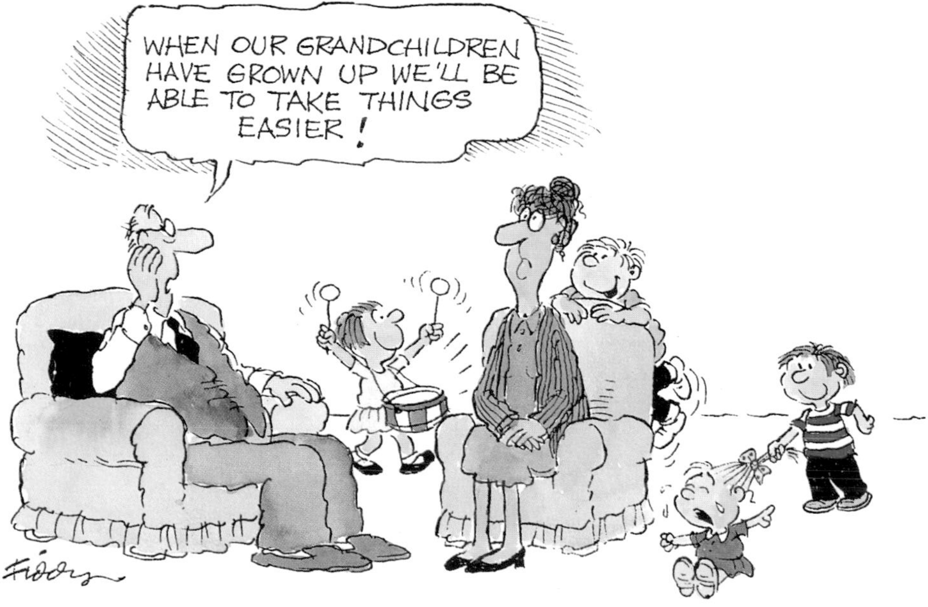
WHEN OUR GRANDCHILDREN HAVE GROWN UP WE'LL BE ABLE TO TAKE THINGS EASIER !
Fiddy

YOU CAN

TAKE UP SITTING AROUND...

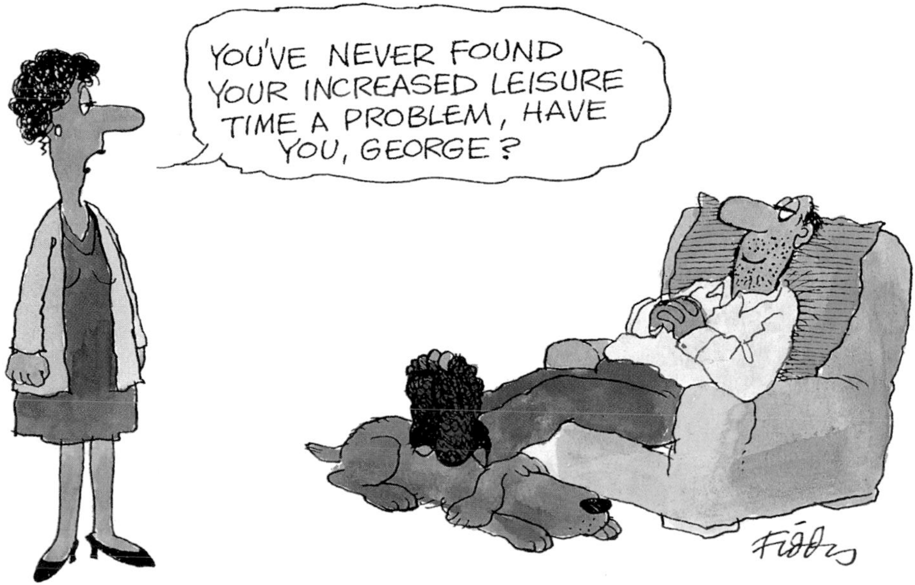
YOU'VE NEVER FOUND YOUR INCREASED LEISURE TIME A PROBLEM, HAVE YOU, GEORGE?

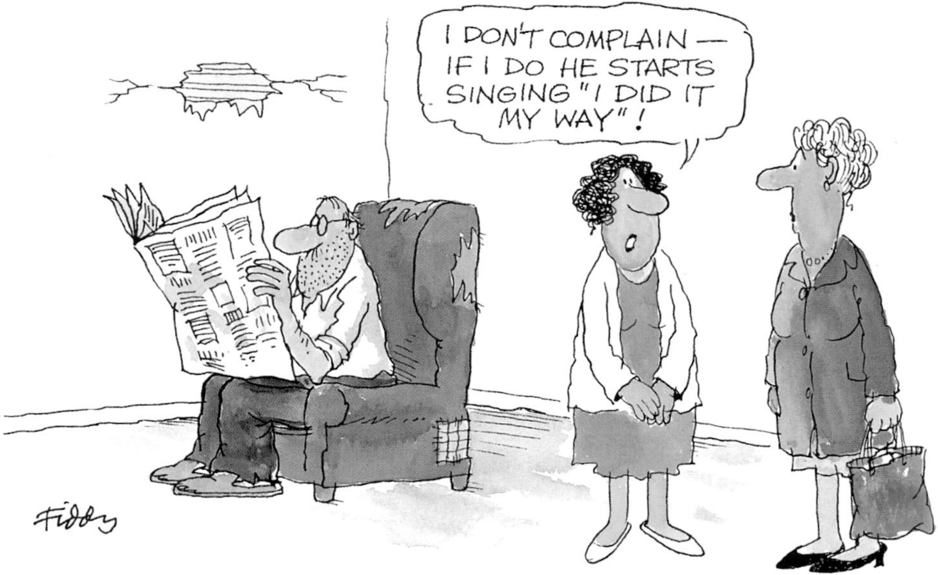
I DON'T COMPLAIN — IF I DO HE STARTS SINGING "I DID IT MY WAY"!
Fiddy

YOU CAN GET CLOSER

—AND DO THINGS TOGETHER...

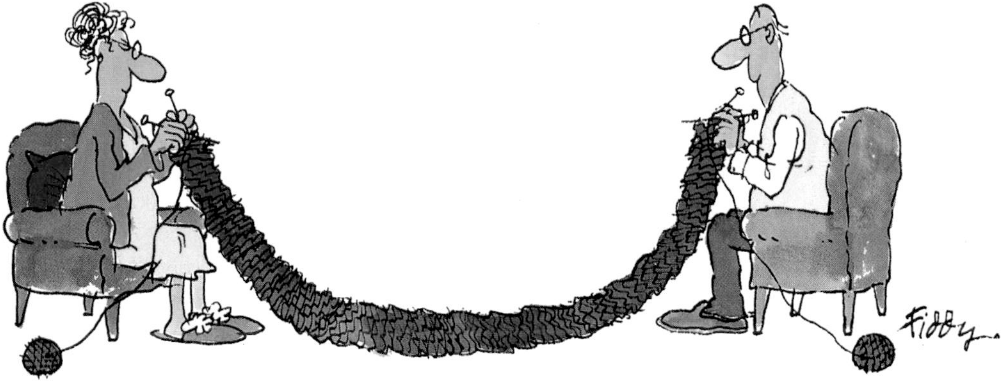
Fiddy

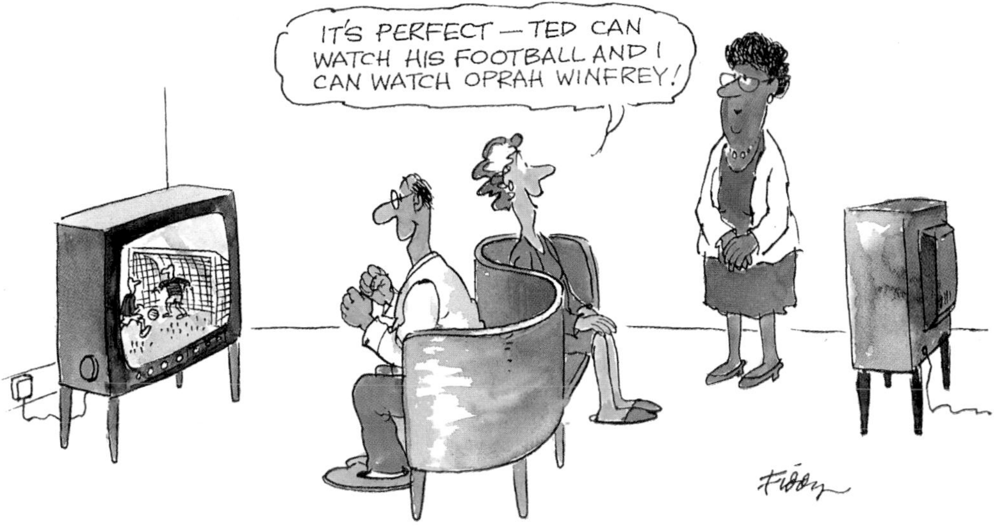
IT'S PERFECT — TED CAN WATCH HIS FOOTBALL AND I CAN WATCH OPRAH WINFREY!
Fiddy

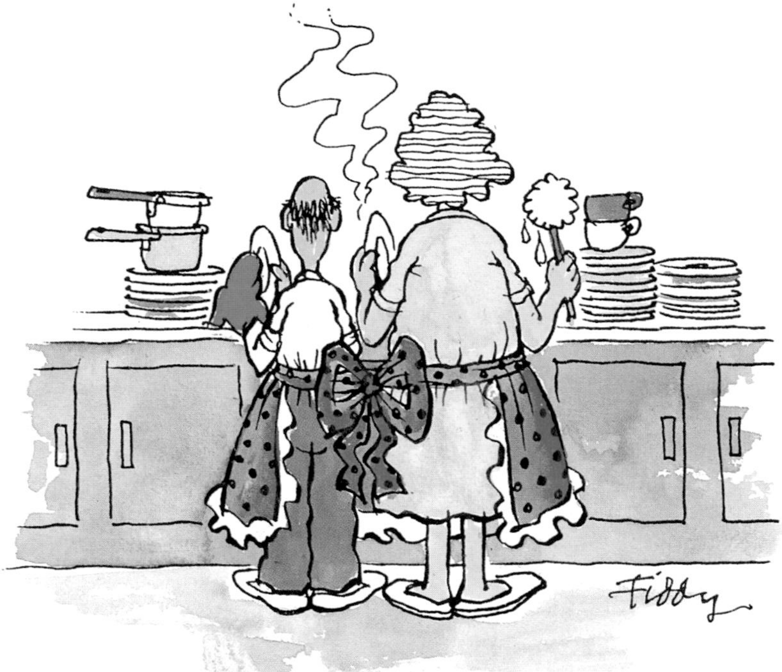
Fiddy

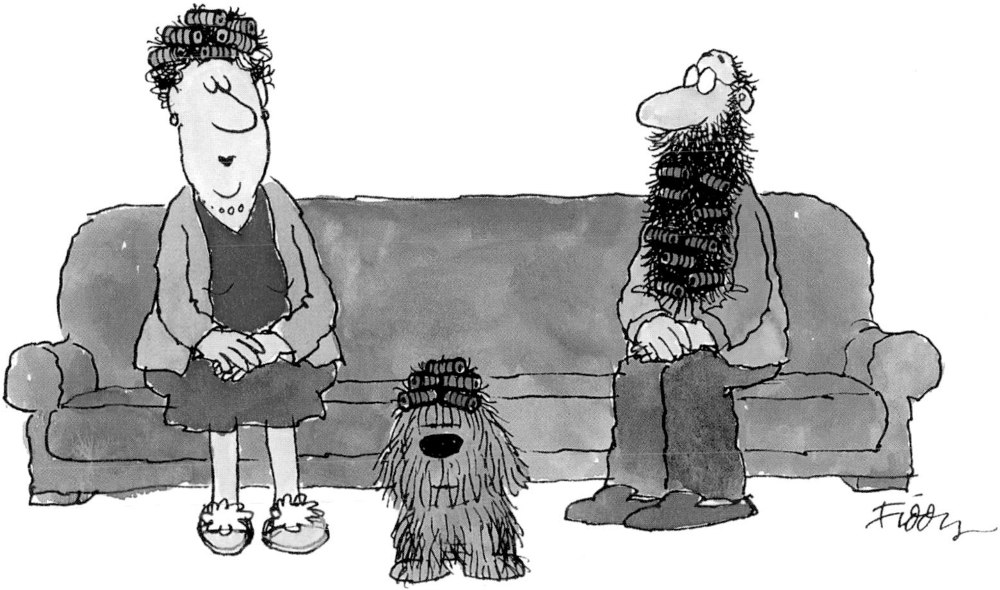
Fiddy

..CURL UP WITH YOUR SWEETIE-PIE

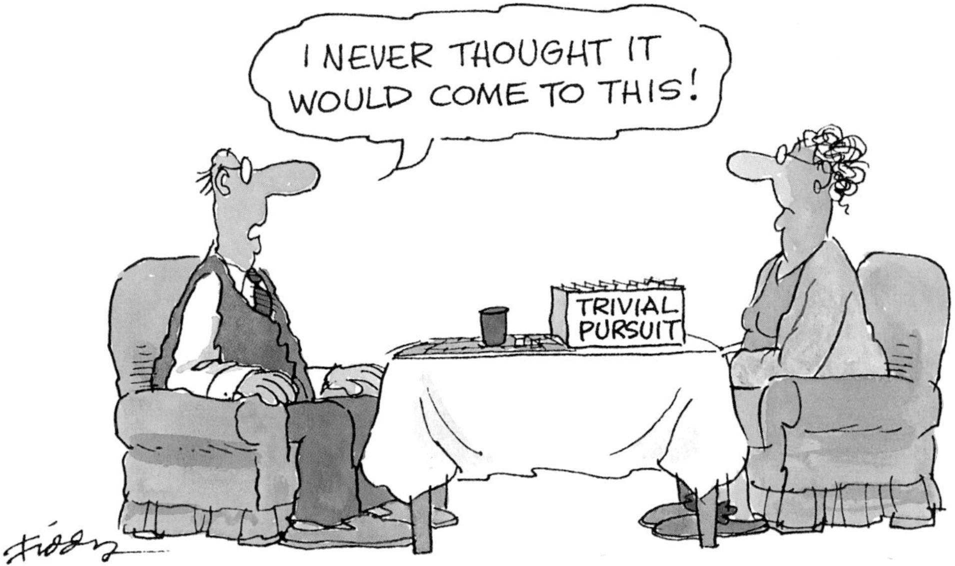
I NEVER THOUGHT IT WOULD COME TO THIS!
TRIVIAL PURSUIT

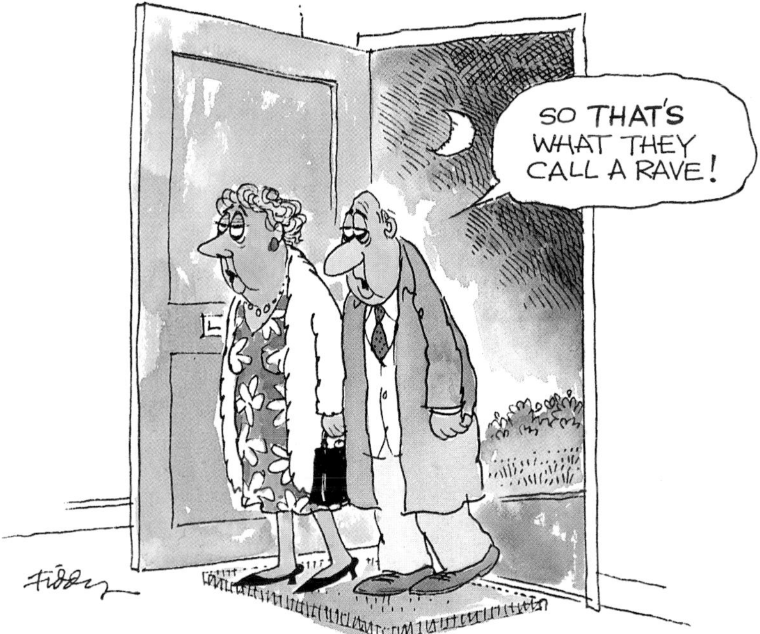
SO THAT'S WHAT THEY CALL A RAVE!

GO FOR IT!
LIVE IT UP!

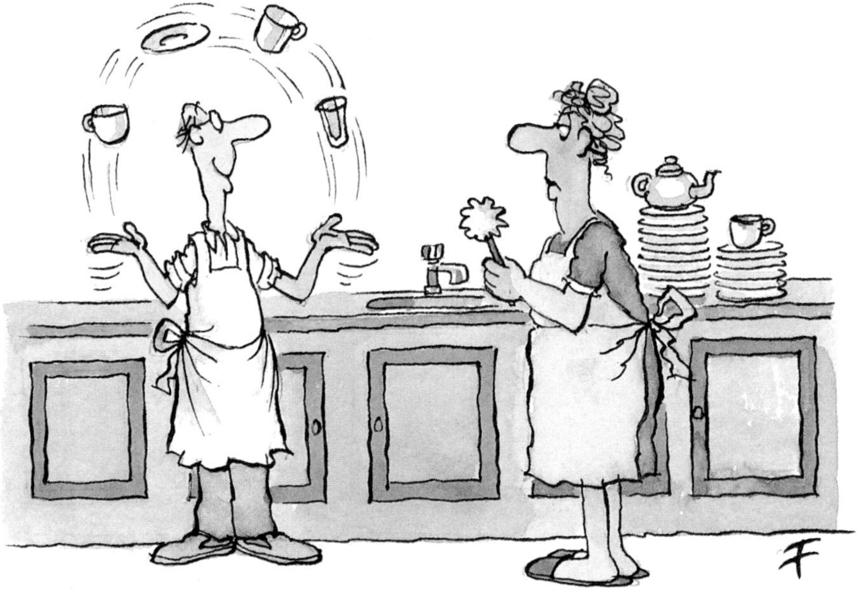

MAKE WASHING UP A FUN TIME

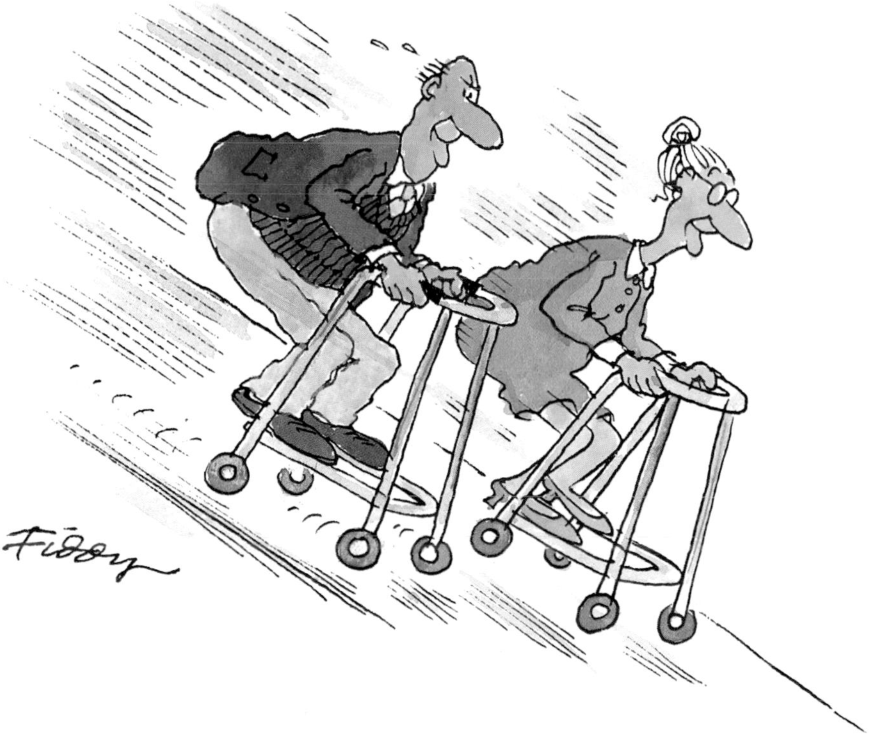

Books in the "Crazy World" series

The Crazy World of Cats (Bill Stott)
The Crazy World of Football (Bill Stott)
The Crazy World of Gardening (Bill Stott)
The Crazy World of Golf (Mike Scott)
The Crazy World of Housework (Bill Stott)
The Crazy World of Marriage (Bill Stott)
The Crazy World of Rugby (Bill Stott)
The Crazy World of Sex (Bill Stott)

Books in the "Fanatic's" series

The Fanatic's Guides are perfect presents for
everyone with a hobby that has got out of hand.
Over fifty hilarious colour cartoons by Roland Fiddy.

The Fanatic's Guide to Cats
The Fanatic's Guide to Computers
The Fanatic's Guide to Dads
The Fanatic's Guide to D.I.Y.
The Fanatic's Guide to Golf
The Fanatic's Guide to Husbands
The Fanatic's Guide to Love
The Fanatic's Guide to Sex

Great Britain: Order these super books from
your local bookseller or from Exley Publications Ltd,
16 Chalk Hill, Watford, Herts WD19 4BG.